Christmas in Bethlehem

A Moravian Heritage

Vangie Roby Sweitzer

Published by Central Moravian Church, 73 West Church Street, Bethlehem, Pennsylvania, 18018

Cover and Interior Designer: Kristen Morgan Downey
Copy Editor: Kathy Diehl Everleth
Produced by Dog's Breakfast

Printed in China

1 3 5 7 9 10 8 6 4 2
First Edition

"Whenever I become jaundiced by relentless reminders of the number of shopping days left until Christmas, by tinny renditions of 'Chestnuts roasting on an open fire,' by over-priced, gold-plated gifts for those who have everything, I stuff my bah humbugs in a sack and head for Bethlehem, PA, where all my doubts are suspended for another year."

"The attraction of Bethlehem is summed up in one word: tradition. Over the years, the city stays the same, quietly making its putzes, molding its beeswax candles, hanging its Herrnhut stars, and, more than anything else, steadfastly recognizing that Christmas is. . .a time for celebration, a time to recall the birth of an infant in another Bethlehem in another time and place. Everything in Moravian life centers on that birth."

"O Little Town in Pennsylvania"
John T. Cunningham
Mid-Atlantic Country, December 1991

CONTENTS

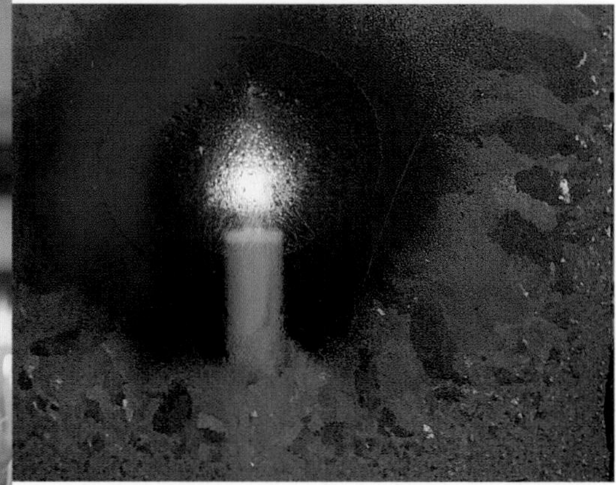

PART II *Bethlehem's Celebration of Christmas and Its Moravian Influence*

ACKNOWLEDGMENTS

IN GRATEFUL APPRECIATION. . .

…to the following benefactors who made the publishing of this book possible:

CENTRAL MORAVIAN CHURCH, BETHLEHEM, PA

The Outreach Grants Committee
The Busy Workers
The Ladies' Sewing Society
The Peanutmakers

BETHLEHEM AREA MORAVIANS, INC.

…for his support of and confidence in this project:

The Rev. Dr. Douglas W. Caldwell, Senior Pastor,
Central Moravian Church

…for her creative talent in design and layout:

Kristen Morgan Downey

…for their generous assistance in editing for historical accuracy:

Susan Dreydoppel, Executive Director, Moravian Historical Society, Nazareth, PA
The Rev. Dr. Albert H. Frank, Assistant Archivist, Moravian Archives, Bethlehem, PA

…for assistance in the creative process:

The Rev. Carol Reifinger, Associate Pastor, Central Moravian Church
Jean Kessler, past member, Board of Directors, Bethlehem Tourism Authority

…for his patience and encouragement:

my husband, Donald, "the wind beneath my wings"

…for finding me invaluable, out-of-print books on the Internet:

our son, Mark

...and to all those who answered my myriad questions:

David Amidon, Professor of Urban Studies, Lehigh University
William Burkhardt, Candlemakers, Edgeboro Moravian Church
Anne Cates, School Secretary, Moravian Academy
John Cornish, Director, Live Bethlehem Christmas Pageant
Debbie Delgrosso, Manager, Moravian Book Shop
Mary Ann Dwyer, Executive Director, Bethlehem Tourism Authority
The Rev. J. Christian Giesler, Chaplain, Moravian College and Theological Seminary
Dr. Daniel Gilbert, Assistant Archivist, Moravian College and Theological Seminary
Jeffrey Griffis, Male Head Sacristan, Central Moravian Church
Jane Hammond, Collections, Moravian Museum
Carol Henn, Executive Director, Lehigh Valley Community Foundation
Susan Hercek, President, Cathedral Choral Society
Marcia Horning, Mintmakers, Edgeboro Moravian Church
Karen Huetter, Director of Educational Services, Historic Bethlehem Partnership
Sarah Jubinski, President, St. Nicholas Russian Orthodox Church
Ruth Kelly, Docent, Moravian Museum
Don Kemmerer, Director, Bethlehem Moravian Trombone Choir
Bertie Knisely, Alumni Director, Moravian College
Alice and Francis Knouss, members, Central Moravian Church
Wendy Martin, Site Supervisor, Kemerer Museum of Decorative Arts
Dessa McCormick, Site Supervisor, Moravian Museum of Bethlehem
Eileen Mera, Chairman, East Hills Moravian Church Putz
Charlene Donchez Mowers, Executive Director, Historic Bethlehem Partnership
Rosemary Murdy-Haber, Director of Choral Music, Freedom High School
The Rev. Vernon Nelson, Executive Director, Moravian Archives
Barbara Parry, Moravian College Alumni Department
Mark Parseghian, Candlemakers, Central Moravian Church
Gloria Reisinger, Secretary to the Provincial Elders Conference, Moravian Church Center
Lydia Roque, Secretary, Holy Infancy Church
Richard and Monica Schantz, Music Directors, Central Moravian Church
Barbara Senick, Assistant Organist, Central Moravian Church
Nancy Shumaker, Director of Choral Music, Liberty High School
Robert W. A. and Lucille Smith, Candlemakers, Central Moravian Church
Kathie Smyser, Mintmakers, Edgeboro Moravian Church
Mrs. Robert S. Taylor, former Moravian Museum Board member
Mark Turdo, Curator, Moravian Historical Society
Paul Turk, Wood Street, Bethlehem Postmaster, U.S. Postal Service

FOREWORD

Welcome to the Christmas City, Bethlehem, Pennsylvania. You are about to learn of and savor Christmas as do tens of thousands of people who make a pilgrimage to this charming community each year.

You will be guided by two Moravians, Vangie Sweitzer and Kristen Downey, who have combined their talents to treat you to a Christmas experience that is uniquely, unforgettably, and distinctively Moravian. They will put you in touch with the original Christmas story, which occurred in Bethlehem of Judea long ago, as you are taken to the putz, as you learn the meaning of the Moravian Star, and as you are escorted into church to worship the Christ child through Scripture, music, and a beeswax candle. There are many other lovely traditions you will read about and observe in the following pages.

Vangie is among the best-qualified to tell the story in her own words. She has been doing it for more than a decade in her role as the Associate Director of the Bethlehem Area Chamber of Commerce, the Director of Tourism for the Chamber, a Docent at the Moravian Museum, as well as caring for public relations at Christmas for the Bethlehem Tourism Authority.

Kristen has interpreted the story skillfully by designing the book as well as editing the numerous photographs that illustrate it. She has esteemed herself as a Senior Book Designer for Rodale Inc., and is currently the Associate Art Director for *Bicycling* magazine.

Apart from their professional skills, they bring integrity to this special Christmas story as women who are also a part of the story as dedicated members of the Moravian Church.

The Rev. Dr. Douglas W. Caldwell
Senior Pastor, Central Moravian Church

PART I

Moravian Christmas Traditions

A MORAVIAN CHRISTMAS

Each Christmas in Bethlehem of Pennsylvania, the sweet smell of beeswax candles fills Moravian church sanctuaries, and voices are joined in one particular hymn of proclamation, "Jesus, Call Thou Me."

The lighting of beeswax candles holds a unique place in the hearts of Moravians everywhere, for it is a tradition that began more than two-and-a-half centuries ago in Germany. To Bethlehem Moravians, the singing of this simple hymn has even more extraordinary meaning.

On Christmas Eve of 1741, Count Nicholas Ludwig von Zinzendorf met with a small band of Moravian settlers for a Communion service in their first house. Moving into the adjoining stable, the congregation sang a hymn that he had chosen, "Jesus, Call Thou Me." Its second verse explains its significance:

"Not Jerusalem—lowly Bethlehem
'Twas that gave us Christ to save us,
Not Jerusalem."

In those moments, Count Zinzendorf christened the new settlement "Bethlehem."

Each Christmas, there is special emotion as Bethlehem Moravians, and many hundreds more from the community, join in lighting beeswax candles and in singing the now-beloved hymn "Jesus, Call Thou Me." For these are traditions that have lived on through more than 250 Christmases.

The Moravians, a Protestant denomination that immigrated to America to spread the Gospel to Native Americans and unchurched Germans, brought many of their customs with them. Through the centuries, other Moravian traditions have

TRADITIONS
A young girl in 18th-century Moravian garb holds a traditional beeswax candle. The Advent star that hangs in Central Moravian Church glows in the background.

O LITTLE TOWN OF BETHLEHEM

Each Christmas season, the city is transformed into a magical place that glows with its extensive yet tasteful holiday lighting.

joined in making the season, and the city, unique. Single lighted electric candles are placed in the windows of every Moravian building and many of their homes, and in those of multitudes of non-Moravians. Illuminated Moravian Stars glow from hundreds of doorways. Lovefeasts are celebrated by Moravian congregations. Moravian community putzes, miniature nativity scenes with lights and narration, are lovingly set in place in three Bethlehem Moravian churches, readied for public viewing by many thousands. Lantern-lit tours of the city's centuries-old streets and buildings are led by guides in Moravian costume. And everywhere, music is heard, voices sing out, trumpets and trombones sound in vespers, vigils, and concerts, in churches, in the college and university, on city streets.

In keeping with its religious heritage, Bethlehem's celebration of the season and its extensive yet simple lighting display begin on the first Sunday of Advent. Late that afternoon, following a Lovefeast in the 1,100-seat Central Moravian Church, members of the congregation and community and visitors who have come to share the traditions converge at City Center Plaza, just one block east of the church. There, during the Community Tree-Lighting Ceremony at dusk, a switch is thrown to illuminate the city's historic north side with thousands of white lights on hundreds of Christmas trees, and the south side with as many colored lights. Over all shines the city's well-known beacon, an 81-foot-high, 53-foot-wide electric star, high atop nearby South Mountain.

Each December, many thousands come to Bethlehem from all over the world to be moved by the heritage and the traditions, to experience what has become known as Christmas City USA, and to share in the sights and sounds of a city steeped in three centuries of history. Within the pages of this book, we celebrate the customs begun by the Moravians and perpetuated by thousands more in surrounding areas. It is these traditions that assure to all who travel here...a very special Christmas.

WHO ARE THE MORAVIANS?

The history of the Moravian Church can be traced back nearly 600 years, with its roots in Prague, in the present-day Czech Republic. Fully 100 years before Martin Luther's Reformation, a Roman Catholic priest named John Hus set out to reform the church. Through careful study of the Scriptures, Hus developed the belief that communication with the common people was of utmost importance. It was his feeling that the truth was in the Gospel, and that only God, through Christ, could forgive one of any sin. He believed that the sermon and Scripture should be in the language of the people, rather than in Latin, and that both bread and wine should be served at Communion. For his beliefs, he was declared a heretic and was burned at the stake on his 46th birthday, July 6, 1415.

CENTRAL CHURCH BELFRY
Bethlehem's most recognizable landmark is the belfry of Central Moravian Church. The church was built in 1803–1806 to seat 1,500 people, when there were only 580 settlers in the entire community.

When he died, Hus left many followers. In 1457, a group of those followers, whose beliefs were centered in the Gospel,

COUNT NICHOLAS LUDWIG VON ZINZENDORF
A well-to-do Lutheran nobleman, Count Zinzendorf, became the patron of the Moravians, offering them a safe haven on his estate in Saxony.

founded a church called the *Unitas Fratrum*, or Unity of the Brethren. The membership of the Brethren rose to more than 200,000. For the next two centuries, Protestants in eastern Europe were widely persecuted. In 1618, the Thirty Years' War broke out, almost eradicating the Brethren. They went underground to worship, praying that God would preserve a "hidden seed" to flourish once more.

In 1722, in Saxony, now eastern Germany, that seed had its opportunity for rebirth. A well-to-do Lutheran nobleman, Count Nicholas Ludwig von Zinzendorf, had heard of these refugees who, by the next decade, began to call themselves Moravians. The term originated as a nickname, since many of the refugees had come from the province of Moravia. Count Zinzendorf, only 22 years old, was intensely interested in religion and had sympathy for these people who had been persecuted for their faith.

Soon, Moravians began to settle on his estate in Saxony. They built a little town there and named it *Herrnhut*, meaning "the Lord's watch." Count Zinzendorf thought that the church might endure for "perhaps 50 years." Instead, the group at Herrnhut prospered. As the Renewed Moravian Church, they pledged to send missionaries "not where the task was easy, but where the need was greatest." They set out to seek "the last, the least, and the lost," traveling to Greenland, to the Caribbean, and to Africa.

Eventually, they reached America. The first ten Moravians settled in and around Savannah, Georgia, in 1735. By 1740, they moved on to Pennsylvania. Their intent was to bring the Gospel of Christ to the Native Americans and unchurched colonists. The Moravians settled temporarily in Nazareth. Within a year, they purchased 500 acres of land at the junction of the Lehigh River and the Monocacy Creek, ten miles from Nazareth. There, they built their first house on a hill just above the creek. It was in that two-room log structure that 14 settlers observed their first Christmas in Bethlehem, with Count Zinzendorf as their guest.

Today, the six Moravian churches of the Bethlehem area claim total membership of about 3,350, with 4,100 more in the Greater Lehigh Valley. The Moravian Church, still officially known as the Unitas Fratrum, remains a small denomination: just over 51,000 members in the United States and Canada and nearly 789,000 worldwide. A regular Protestant denomination in the mainstream of Christianity, the Moravian Church is the oldest organized Protestant church in the world. It is Christ-centered in its beliefs, and is truly a worldwide church.

THE NAMING OF BETHLEHEM

It was Christmas Eve of 1741. The Moravians in the new Pennsylvania settlement were filled with excitement and a great sense of anticipation as they awaited a visit from their patron in Europe, Count Nicholas Ludwig von Zinzendorf.

The previous winter, they had purchased 500 acres of land on the northern bank of the Lehigh River, near the Monocacy Creek. That spring, on a slope just east of the creek, they had built their first house. It was a two-room structure of square-hewn logs, with one end serving as a stable, the rest as the residence for this first group of settlers.

THE FIRST HOUSE
This painting by Gustav Grunewald, a 19th-century Moravian, shows the humble cabin where the settlers celebrated their first Christmas Eve in 1741.

Late in the winter of 1741, they had begun work on a much larger building, a *Gemeinhaus*, or community house, just 100 yards east of the first house. Throughout that summer and fall, work on the Gemeinhaus continued. Although it was not complete as Christmas of 1741 approached, it was far enough

GEMEINHAUS

Built in 1741, the Gemeinhaus is the oldest building standing in Bethlehem, Pennsylvania.

along to accommodate some of its builders, as well as Count Zinzendorf. He had arrived in New York that month with a small party that included his daughter, Countess Benigna, and several others. After a brief stay in Philadelphia, the Count and his fellow travelers set out for the new Moravian colony.

Toward evening on December 24, the small congregation gathered to receive Holy Communion. Hours later, the scene was described by Martin Mack, one of the original settlers, in his *Autobiography.* "While celebrating the vigils of Christmas-eve in the first house, and as we were closing the services (it was already past nine o'clock), the Count led the way into the stable that adjoined our dwelling and commenced singing the hymn that opens with the words, '*Nicht Jerusalem, sondern Bethlehem, aus dir kommet was mir frommet....*'"

The first three verses of this Epiphany hymn written by Adam Drese a half-century earlier translate from German as follows:

Jesus, call Thou me,
from the world to thee;
Speed me ever, stay me never;
Jesus, call Thou me.

Not Jerusalem—lowly Bethlehem
'Twas that gave us Christ to save us;
Not Jerusalem.

Favored Bethlehem!
honored is that name;
Thence came Jesus to release us;
Favored Bethlehem.

It was a Moravian tradition to name communities before they were settled, and to use biblical names. In Hebrew, Bethlehem translates to *Beth-Lechem*, or "House of Bread." By coincidence, *Lecha* is a German abbreviation of the Lenape name for the Lehigh River; thus "house on the Lehigh" could then designate the location of the settlement.

And so it was that as the small band of Moravians gathered that evening in their humble cabin, Count Zinzendorf publicly christened the tiny settlement "Bethlehem."

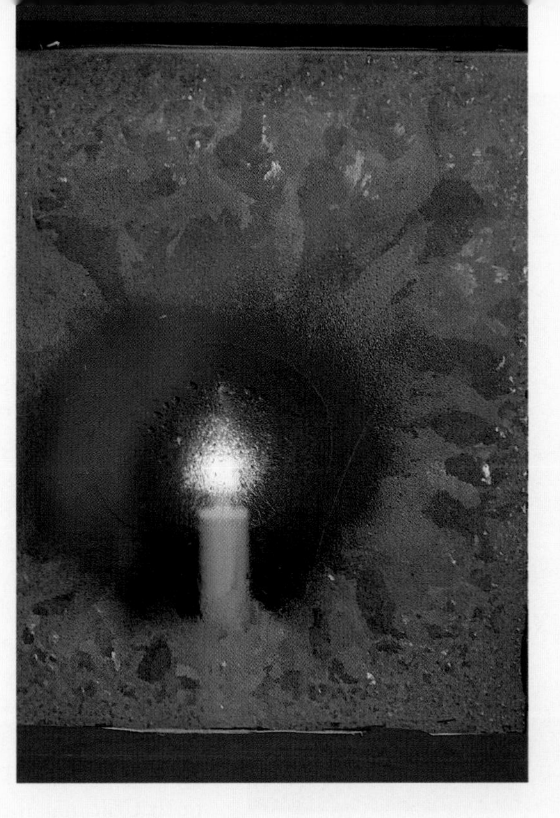

A CANDLE IN EVERY WINDOW

One of Bethlehem's best-loved and most beautiful traditions is the custom of placing a single lighted candle in each window of thousands of buildings throughout the area. It is an arresting sight. But how did it all begin?

While the narrative of Count Zinzendorf's visit to the new Moravian settlement on the Lehigh River in December of 1741 has been told and told again, lesser-known are the reports of the many pilgrim settlements developed by him in Europe. One such settlement in Germany was Herrnhaag, where a building was erected for Count Zinzendorf and called *Lichtenburg*, or "Castle of Light." During the Advent season, every window would be lighted with a candle to welcome the Christ child.

CHRISTMAS CANDLE
As a distinctively Christian symbol, the candle has been used to represent three main ideas: Christ as the Light of the world, the Bible as the inspired word of God, and the church as shining for God in the world.

In later years, a large number of this Herrnhaag congregation journeyed to Bethlehem as the second sea congregation. (Each group of Moravians traveling to America during that period had a minister on board the ship, thus the term *sea congregation*.) Undoubtedly, the group had memories of that early tradition, but documentation of that symbolic gesture being upheld in Bethlehem does not appear until the late 1920s, when Dr. Edwin Heath, president of the Moravian Seminary and College for Women, and his wife, Mabel, began the custom of placing a lighted beeswax candle in each window of the Single Brethren's House (then known as Colonial Hall) on Christmas Eve. By the late 1930s, the windows of both Colonial and Main Halls on South Campus were illuminated by a safer and more enduring method, 101 lighted electric candles. These were lit at the beginning of Advent and continued through Epiphany, welcoming all visitors to the Moravians' historic buildings. Eventually, the custom spread to the college's North Campus as well.

In 1937, the Bethlehem Chamber of Commerce began to publicize Bethlehem nationwide as "Christmas City USA," and both the city itself and the community's residents initiated a massive lighting display. By 1940, the tradition that is now known as "A Single Candle in Every Window" had spread further through the city, not only in Moravian buildings but also in businesses and homes throughout the area.

Today, the custom has spread beyond the bounds of Moravian tradition. Candles now glow in windows on block after block of Bethlehem streets, and miles beyond. For

the most part, residents, businesses, and public buildings light their candles on the first Sunday evening of Advent and continue the practice through Epiphany Sunday. The Star on South Mountain leads modern-day pilgrims to Bethlehem of Pennsylvania—the candles' glow welcomes them as they arrive.

In observing this tradition, each one reflects, in his or her own belief, a sign of welcome to the Christ child and a symbol of warmth and hospitality to the stranger who passes by.

Clockwise from above

SLEEMAN HOME, BRETHREN'S HOUSE, SCHADT HOME

"Charming in its utter simplicity, Moravian's contribution to Bethlehem, the Christmas City, was the lighting of 101 electric candles in its windows each night during the Yuletide season. The thousands of visitors who flocked to the city were profoundly impressed by the observance of this custom."

Excerpt from *Alumnae Bulletin*
Moravian Seminary and College for Women
March 1939

THE MORAVIAN STAR

A star as a symbol of Christ's birth is as old as the event itself. While there is nothing unique in the use of the star as a Christmas decoration, one particular form of star has become associated with the way the Moravian Church celebrates Christmas. Thus, one of the most familiar sights during the Advent and Christmas season is what is known as the Moravian Star. Illuminated from within, it hangs on porches, in doorways, and in windows throughout the city of Bethlehem and beyond.

The star is hung in Moravian churches on the first Sunday of Advent and precedes all other Christmas decorations. For that reason, it is also called the Advent Star. Still another name for it is the Herrnhut Star because for many years, it was manufactured exclusively in Herrnhut, Germany, the town established by early Moravians on Count Zinzendorf's estate.

Originally, the star was a product of handicraft sessions of the Moravian boys' school in Niesky, Germany, about 1850. It began as an experiment in geometry, gradually becoming an art form. About 1900, Pieter Verbeeck, who had attended the boys' school in Niesky and was proprietor of a paper and music store in Herrnhut, began to produce the stars for sale in his home. His son, Harry, later founded a company in Herrnhut that would make the stars, and they quickly began to supply stars to Moravians in Europe, America, and throughout the mission fields.

ADVENT STAR
Bethlehem's largest Moravian Star hangs in the sanctuary of Central Moravian Church. The star is hung in Moravian churches for the first Sunday of Advent and precedes all other holiday decorations.

The Moravian Star is a familiar sight both in churches and in homes. Its use has spread to businesses and public buildings. In Bethlehem, the largest Moravian Star hangs in the sanctuary of Central Moravian Church at the corner of Main and Church

A WELCOMING TRADITION
Advent Stars, also known as Moravian Stars or Herrnhut Stars, glow in the doorways of homes within the Historic District, throughout the city of Bethlehem and beyond.

Streets. The second-largest, and the most visible to the community, is the star that hangs outside the entry to Summit Bank at the corner of Broad and New Streets in the Historic District.

Today, stars are made of paper, plastic, and leaded glass. They can be obtained in many sizes, with the most common number of points being 26.

The Moravian Star cannot help but remind us of the star that led the wise men from their home in the distant East to Bethlehem, where they presented gifts to the Christ child. Many interpret the multiple points of the star as a reminder that we should follow Christ's command, going into all corners of the world, spreading the Gospel and baptizing in His name.

THE MORAVIAN PUTZ

Many who visit Bethlehem during the Christmas season declare that they have come to find the real meaning of Christmas. Nowhere is the spirit of the season more readily captured than in the Community Putz located in each of three Bethlehem Moravian churches.

The word *putz* is derived from the old German term *putzen*, which means "to arrange" or "to decorate." In this uniquely Moravian tradition, miniature nativity figures are arranged in scenes with common materials such as moss, bark, stones, and stumps of trees enhancing the creation of the putz. Even these simple items may have sentimental value to those who have collected the materials over many years. Animals, villages, and streams of water add further authenticity.

MARY AND JOSEPH
The familiar figures of Mary and Joseph are depicted in miniature in the Community Putz at East Hills Moravian Church.

The idea for the creation of a putz apparently originated in churches of the Middle Ages, when priests placed figures of the

THE CHRISTMAS STORY

Hand-carved wooden figurines tell the story of the birth of Jesus in this scene from Central Moravian Church's Community Putz.

"You might spend a hundred dollars upon one (putz), which would not be worth a dime in real value. It must be yourself."

"The background and the real meaning of the Christmas putz is one of those intangible assets of a community's life that can never be wholly replaced by a substitute. It is an annual expression of that higher and better side of ourselves, which we hope that our children may remember of us. It is one of the things that make up Christmas, the real Christmas, for it keeps us linked with the one radiant truth, that through the Nativity of Christ there came to us all the light and life that the world knows."

Excerpts of remarks by the late A. D. Thaeler, D.D., made during an address to the Bethlehem Women's Club, Christmas 1926. The Rev. Dr. Thaeler was pastor of Central Moravian Church from 1901 to 1918.

Holy Family in churches to give those who were less educated a clearer meaning of the Christmas story. Later, it continued in private homes. When the Moravians came to America, many brought with them the cherished figures passed down through generations. Sometimes an entire room of a home, such as a sun porch or entry hall, would be devoted to the building of a putz. In every case, it reflected the artistry of those who fashioned it and was meant for the enjoyment of family, friends, and all those who visited. Not only were the scenes elaborate but their showing was often accompanied by lights and narration.

In Moravian homes, the putz was never viewed by the children in the family until after the Christmas Eve Vigil. Then, the doors to the room designated for the putz would be thrown open so that the children could revel in the wonders of each tiny scene. Presents would be opened, and the Christmas season would begin.

In the late 19th century and early 20th century in Bethlehem, the days between Christmas and Twelfth Night, or Epiphany, were looked upon as a great social time of putz parties. During evening open houses, families would "go putzing" to one another's homes. At each home, they would enjoy the creativity of the scenes as they partook of special treats such as Moravian sugar or spice cookies along with a beverage.

At one point in the mid 1930s, nearly 1,000 people came to the door of the Edward Neisser home, wishing to view his elaborate putz. Neisser then suggested that a putz be built in Central Moravian Church, and for a short time, a small one was constructed on the second floor, just above the pulpit area of the church.

In December 1937, Bethlehem celebrated its most elaborate Christmas. The Bethlehem Chamber of Commerce had decided to proclaim to the entire nation that, hereafter, Bethlehem would be known as "Christmas City USA." At the same time, it asked Central Moravian Church to create a community putz. That Christmas, the Moravians built a putz in the Main Street office of the Chamber of Commerce. Fourteen thousand people visited the putz over four weeks, making it difficult for the Chamber to carry on its business.

The next year, in 1938, a large putz was constructed in the Hotel Bethlehem. Two hundred people took turns reading the narration and operating the lights. That Christmas, 40,000 people came to view the putz, representing two-thirds of the states of the United States and eight foreign countries. Obviously overwhelmed, the hotel asked the Moravians to find still another new home for their popular attraction.

After one year (1939) in the gymnasium of Moravian Seminary and College for Women (today known as Payne Gallery), the putz was moved to the Central Moravian Sunday School building, now called the Christian Education building. After a series of changes and interruptions during the years of World War II, the putz resumed in the Christian Education building in 1946 under the supervision of the Service Guild, later called Central Moravian Women's Fellowship. The women assumed the awesome task of recruiting volunteers to assist in the month-long showing of the putz through 1997. Today, an expanded Putz Committee, under the direction of the church's Board of Elders, supervises both the building of the putz annually

EDGEBORO MORAVIAN COMMUNITY PUTZ

A broad view shows the many scenes depicted through lights and narration. A traditional Moravian Star hangs over all.

and the assignments of volunteers.

Each year, Central's putz has its beginnings on a moss-gathering Sunday early in November. Members of the congregation travel to the Pocono Mountains to gather moss, which forms the base of the putz. Construction, later in November, takes about a week. Today, as in centuries past, the building of the putz may be thought of as a form of artistry. Entire families participate, and while the biblical narration remains the same, the placement of the scenes and tiny figures varies according to individual tastes from year to year.

Numerous times daily from the first Sunday of Advent through New Year's Day, the Christmas story is narrated in a darkened auditorium, as one small scene after another is lighted. A hush falls over the room as young and old focus on the words of the age-old Christmas story and the tiny figures that depict it. A sense of wonder envelops those who view it, and many exclaim as the brief presentation concludes, "I feel like I've heard the Christmas story for the first time."

In Bethlehem, the three Moravian Community Putzes draw many thousands of visitors each year. The putz at Central Moravian Church is the oldest, in existence since 1937. East Hills Moravian Church has welcomed visitors to their putz since 1980, and Edgeboro Moravian Church introduced their community putz in 1988. Each in its own way, these three churches use this uniquely Moravian tradition as an outreach ministry to the community. In both preparation and presentation, it is truly a labor of love for the hundreds who volunteer their services to share with the Bethlehem community this most cherished Moravian tradition.

THE MORAVIAN BEESWAX CANDLE

To Moravians around the world, the tradition of using lighted candles in Christmas Eve Vigils is time-honored. The beautiful custom originated in 1747, when Bishop John de Watteville introduced it in Marienborn Castle, Germany, during a service for children living there. Long before that, Moravians had purposely made much of Christmas. They looked upon it both as a festival celebrating a central Christian truth and as an occasion when children particularly could learn what the birth of the Christ child in Bethlehem meant for the world.

BEESWAX CANDLES
The candle, or taper, is a religious symbol of great antiquity that can be traced back to pre-Christian days.

On Christmas Eve of 1747, Bishop de Watteville shared these thoughts and spoke of the happiness that we share as a result of Christ's birth, passion, and wounds and of His kindling a little blood-red flame in each believing heart thereby. To

help the children remember this, each was given a burning candle wrapped with a red ribbon.

By the following Christmas, the church in Herrnhut had adopted the practice. Since then, it has spread wherever Moravians have gone. When they came to America, they brought with them the custom of using lighted candles in children's Christmas Eve Vigils. The first reference to the use of candles in this country is in Bethlehem in 1756.

According to American Moravian tradition, the candles in many churches of this denomination are made of beeswax, which most properly represents the sinless purity of Christ. When lit, the taper reminds us that Christ is the Light of the world. Because the beeswax candle has been such a recognizable symbol of the Moravian Church for more than 250 years, some congregations initiate "beeswax candle evangelism"—delivering these fragrant candles door-to-door, as a way of acquainting neighbors with special Christmas services.

Central Moravian Church molds and trims 10,000 beeswax candles for each Christmas season. The method of carrying out this tradition is much the same as it has been for more than two centuries. For many years, the making of the candles has begun on the Tuesday after Labor Day and continues each Tuesday of September. More than a dozen Candlemakers take part in the process, representing West Side, College Hill, and Central Moravian Churches. Aluminum alloy molds that have seen this preparation through many Christmas seasons are used.

Once the candles have been molded, another group of volunteers takes on the task of trimming the candles with red fireproof tissue paper. This process takes three to five weeks of meeting each Monday evening. When properly cut and twirled around the candle, the paper creates an attractive ruff that protects the holder of a lighted candle from dripping wax.

An additional two dozen volunteers at Edgeboro Moravian Church trim and mold another 9,000 standard 6-inch beeswax candles throughout October and November. Using antique molds, they also prepare 18-inch candles as special orders for Advent wreaths. Other, older molds accommodate their making of 10-inch candles for home use.

Central Moravian Church keeps half of the 10,000 candles they prepare each year, with 3,300 of them designated for Christmas Eve Vigils. The remainder fills orders received from Moravian churches as near as the Lehigh Valley and as far away as Labrador. They are sent to New York City churches and to others in the Caribbean Islands. They also supply Moravian Academy and Moravian Theological Seminary with candles for their Christmas services as well as for other programs of the church.

Edgeboro Moravian Church's candles are sent as far as the Virgin Islands in addition to nearer churches in New York and Pennsylvania. Many of those they prepare are supplied to the Moravian Book Shop for retail sales. Seven hundred and fifty candles are for use in their own church's Christmas Eve Vigils.

Of all the lights that glow in Bethlehem during the Christmas season, none has more special meaning or a longer history of tradition than the beeswax candle.

Above
BEESWAX DEMONSTRATION
Members of Central Moravian Church, Lucille and Robert Smith, make community appearances in colonial Moravian dress as they demonstrate the making and trimming of beeswax candles.

Opposite page
SPLIT-SECOND TIMING
Trays of candles are lighted just moments before the sacristans' entrance into the sanctuary on Christmas Eve.

VICIT·AGNUS·NOSTER
EUM·SEQUAMUR
HYMNS
for the
Lovefeast on the First Sunday in Advent

THE MORAVIAN LOVEFEAST

A favorite service among Moravians is the Lovefeast, observed twice during the Christmas season at Bethlehem's Central Moravian Church. Traditionally, this church's first Lovefeast observance is held annually on the first Sunday of Advent at 3:30 P.M. The second is the Children's Lovefeast, celebrated at 1:00 P.M. on Christmas Eve. Many tourists as well as local Moravians attend the first of the two. For the second, every seat in the massive sanctuary is filled, as more than 1,000 worshippers of all ages come together to honor the birth of Christ.

The Lovefeast service has its roots in Herrnhut, Germany. On August 13, 1727, a group of refugees from Bohemia and Moravia, now part of the Czech Republic, were assembled in the church at Berthelsdorf. An especially moving Communion service resulted in a tremendous outpouring of God's Spirit, in a manner reminiscent of the day of Pentecost. As worshippers gathered after the service to recount the blessings they had received and draw satisfaction from the broken friendships that had been mended, the young Count Zinzendorf was inspired to send food to several houses in the community. At these homes, members of the congregation might enjoy a simple meal together, an "agape" feast, similar to a shared meal among the early Christians. Thus, the name "lovefeast." This particular date has become known as the Spiritual Birthday of the Renewed Moravian Church.

At Central Church's Advent Lovefeast, after an opening hymn and prayer, women sacristans dressed in white and wearing miniature lace hats, or *haubes*, pass baskets of sweet rolls to the rows of worshippers. The male sacristans then pass among the congregants with trays of coffee mugs. When all have been served, the worshippers partake of the simple meal as the choir offers its anthems.

LOVEFEAST
An expressive vignette displays the program for Central Moravian Church's traditional Advent Lovefeast, with the symbolic bun and mug of coffee.

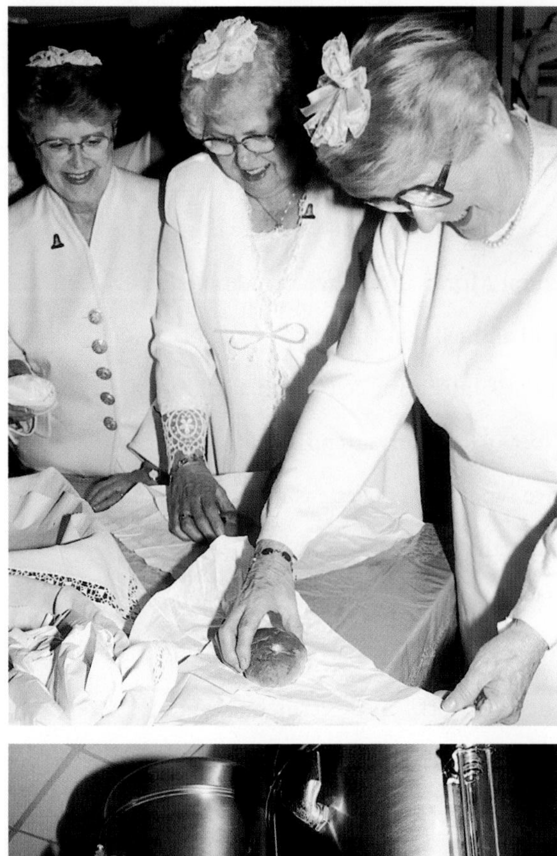

SACRISTANS PREPARE. . .

Female sacristans wrap each bun—a sweet roll with raisins—in a napkin. Urns of coffee await pouring into the mugs by the male sacristans.

. . .WORSHIPPERS PARTAKE
Female sacristans serve the congregration sweet rolls with raisins wrapped in white napkins. In some Moravian churches, sacristans are called *dieners*, German for server.

While first-time visitors may be startled by the serving of buns and coffee during the course of a worship service in the sanctuary, they are often impressed by the unique blend of dignity and informality. An example of a Moravian *singstunde*, or song service, the Lovefeast is made up principally of singing, by both the congregation and by the choir.

The singing of hymns resumes after the brief repast, and the spirit of Christian fellowship lingers. Following the benediction, many of the congregation take time to observe still another Bethlehem tradition: proceeding one block up Church Street to City Center Plaza for the city's Community Tree-Lighting Ceremony.

THE MORAVIAN CHILDREN'S LOVEFEAST

It was during the children's Christmas Vigils at Marienborn in 1747 that Bishop John de Watteville introduced what has become the traditional Moravian Candle Service. In Bethlehem, the Christmas Eve Lovefeast is as old as its earliest congregation, but in 1742, the settlement contained few children. During the Christmas Lovefeast of 1744, however, "a brother sang several hymns for the children that were present." This account from the Bethlehem Diary also records that by the following year, a special Christmas Lovefeast would be held for them.

Most of the 1,100 tickets that are available for the 1:00 P.M. Children's Lovefeast at Central Moravian Church on Christmas Eve are spoken for quickly. While there is no charge for the tickets, they are a necessity in order to assure seats for the three Christmas Eve services held at Central, Bethlehem's first congregation. Only at the children's service is Lovefeast served on Christmas Eve. Anticipation for what is to come combines with the normal clamor to be expected when hundreds of little ones gather, resulting in a rather noisy preamble to the service itself. It is, after all, a service for children.

The attention of many is drawn to the

TRADITIONAL MUGS OF COFFEE

Mugs of coffee with sugar and cream are served by the male sacristans to complete the non-sacramental "breaking of bread" known as Lovefeast.

Family Bell Choir as it rings out its prelude. Then, from children to grandparents, the congregation joins in singing hymns chosen for their words that relate the message of Christ's coming. Throughout the service, congregational hymn singing alternates with anthems sung by children and youth from Central Church and the Lower School of Moravian Academy. Women sacristans pass through the aisles with baskets from which the worshippers draw fat sugar cookies wrapped in white napkins. Male sacristans follow with trays of chocolate milk. While the congregation partakes, anthems are sung by the youth choir.

Finally, it is time for the beloved "Morning Star." For more than 100 years, this hymn has been sung in antiphonal style—since early in the 20th century, by the congregation and a child soloist. Befitting the honor bestowed upon the chosen child, he or she stands centered at the front of the balcony, holding a lighted candle. And then it is time for the high point of the afternoon. With the strains of "Behold, a great, a heavenly light from Bethlehem's manger shining bright. . .," the massive doors at the front of the sanctuary are thrown open, and row after row of sacristans enter, bearing trays of lighted beeswax candles. Quickly, the candles are distributed until all have received one. The closing hymn, "How Bright Appears the Morning Star" is sung, and the benediction is pronounced.

A Massachusetts resident who remains a member of Central Church echoes the general sentiment of many as she sums up the cherished Christmas experience: "When I was a child, I attended Children's Lovefeast with my grandmothers. Now, my family comes home to Bethlehem to attend with their grandmother—my mother. We represent three generations, and even though my children are teenagers now, we continue to attend the afternoon Lovefeast rather than the evening Christmas Eve Vigils. It is a nostalgic experience, a long-time tradition."

And so it has been since 1745.

CHRISTMAS EVE IN BETHLEHEM

It is Christmas Eve in Bethlehem, Pennsylvania. The shops have closed by late afternoon. The doors of museums and other city attractions have not opened on Christmas Eve and Christmas Day. Those who staff them are celebrating this brief time in their own quiet ways. The greatest flurry of the early afternoon is created by late shoppers on historic Main Street and by those arriving for the Moravian Children's Lovefeast.

CANDLES RAISED HIGH
In the final stately strains of the last hymn at Central Church's Christmas Eve Vigils, the congregation's voices swell as 1,000 candles are raised high.

And then, dusk falls. Throughout the Bethlehem area, six Moravian churches have prepared to welcome members and visitors to their traditional Christmas Eve services. On these pages, we focus on just one, Bethlehem's earliest church, with its current edifice that is the third place of worship for the early

Moravian settlers. It is located immediately across the street from the site of that 1741 log cabin, where their first Christmas Eve was observed and where Bethlehem was named more than 250 years ago. It is this historical significance that draws many each Christmas Eve to Central Moravian Church, America's oldest Moravian church.

First, in the hour before 5:30, and then, before 8:00 P.M., a line begins to form on the narrow lane, Heckewelder Place, as worshippers begin their chilly wait for the doors of the church to open. Tickets are necessary to gain admittance; the free tickets assure that there will be adequate seating for the popular services, listed in *USA Today*, December 18, 1998, as one of the "Ten Great Places to Reflect on Christmas Eve." Members of the church, their visiting families, and others from the community and from across the country join in the worship setting.

THE SETTING

Once seated in the dimly lit sanctuary, those present are quickly brought to a sense of quiet worship by the setting itself. The upper pulpit area of the church has been transformed (for the Sunday before Christmas) into a stable reminiscent of the Bethlehem of so long ago. Flanked on either side by large, unadorned fir trees, a massive painted mural of the Nativity fills the apse. At its highest point, long, wooden planks hold back the hay that spills across the width of its vaulted roof. Original gas lamps flicker on the side walls of the sanctuary; a Christmas wreath hangs from each. High above, a huge Moravian Star casts its yellow glow over the heads of the congregation.

The Nativity painting features the Holy Family with shepherds who have come to worship. Research conducted by the Moravian Historical Society in Nazareth seems to indicate that an original mural of the present painting was by Charles Wollmuth, a decorative artist who opened a business in Bethlehem. The mural first appeared in the sanctuary in 1891 as a special decoration for the 150th anniversary of the naming of Bethlehem in 1741. According to speculation, the original mural has been replaced with a copy at least once, as the old one wore out.

The Historical Society reports that it is likely that the original Wollmuth painting was heavily inspired by the work of Moravian painter Gustav Grunewald, and even, perhaps, by similar paintings of the Nativity by John Jacob Mueller (Count Zinzendorf's secretary) or John Valentine Haidt, another noted Moravian painter. Society records point to a close comparison of the original 1891 mural in Central Church with Grunewald's painting of the Nativity. The comparison (of reproductions) indicates that, while the figures are arranged quite differently, the details of the stable and background are strikingly similar.

Definitive information on the painting itself may not be complete, but one thing is certain: As one reflects on the scene, the viewer may realize that he or she seems to

AN AGE-OLD NATIVITY SCENE
Flanked by large, unadorned fir trees, a massive painted mural of the Nativity fills the apse in Central Church. The original mural first appeared in the sanctuary in 1891 as a special decoration for the 150th anniversary of the naming of Bethlehem in 1741.

LIGHT BREAKS FORTH

In the moments before entering the sanctuary, sacristans at Central Moravian Church light the candles. Their entrance, bearing tray after tray of flaming beeswax candles, is met with great anticipation by the Christmas Eve worshippers.

be inside the stable, present at the foot of the newborn babe's manger. It brings a sense of peace, a feeling that one is very near to that first Holy night.

THE SERVICE

It may be said that much of Moravian tradition has been adopted as such by the simple process of "We've always done it that way." Such is certainly the case on Christmas Eve in Central Church. The basic format of the service remains much the same from year to year.

The prelude as worshippers gather has been performed in recent years by guest artists, the Philadelphia Brass, the Concerto Soloists of Philadelphia, and the Moravian College Music Faculty. As the service commences, each hymn, anthem, and chorale that has been chosen weaves together a framework for the birth of Christ. It begins with the far-off tones of the Trombone Choir playing the stately chorale, "Briesen," or "All My Heart This Night Rejoices" (1784), from the attic, 60 feet above the sanctuary. Then the choir renders three verses of "Stille Nacht" in German, often in the lilting setting of Franz Gruber's 1820s composition for a Christmas Eve service in Salzburg, Austria.

The opening strains of the hymn "Jesus, Call Thou Me" are familiar ones, for it is the hymn chosen by Count Zinzendorf on another memorable Christmas Eve. For more than 250 years, it has been sung at Christmastime, and as the congregation repeats the words once again, "Not Jerusalem—lowly Bethlehem 'twas that gave us Christ to save us...," their thoughts may travel across Main Street to the site where those first 14 founders met with Count Zinzendorf and his party on that first Christmas Eve in 1741.

The reading of the age-old Christmas story follows a prayer and a brief welcome by the pastors. At that point, the service becomes a Moravian *singstunde*, or song service, as hymns and anthems echo the Scriptures in song. The 55-voice choir and chamber orchestra have perfected several intricate anthems. Often, a favorite of the congregation is included, Mendelssohn's "There Shall a Star Come Out of Jacob."

Most of the hymns in the Christmas Eve service remain the same from year to year, as tradition takes precedence over variety. Again, a hymn such as "O blessed night without compare on earth...," written by Zinzendorf in 1742 for the settlers' first Christmas Eve in the Gemeinhaus, causes one to speculate as to how many times this hymn has been repeated by earlier Moravians through the centuries.

The first moment of anticipation comes with the singing of "Morning Star" by the child soloist, choir, and congregation. And then the sanctuary darkens. The first and second verses of "Welcome, blessed heavenly stranger, open, Holy Ghost, mine eyes..." conclude quickly, and there is a majestic swell of the organ, a moment of intense expectancy. With the first words of the third verse, "Praise the Lord whose saving splendor shines into the darkest night...," the great doors at the front of the sanctuary swing open, and 20 pairs of sacristans process, the men bearing trays of beeswax candles. It is a breathtaking sight.

Each succeeding hymn speaks of the Light of Christ, and within minutes, the vast sanctuary gains back its light as the female sacristans set the flames aglow one by one, passing them into the pews. When all of the more than 1,000 lighted candles have been passed, the organ swells once again into the final hymn, one of unusual distinction, strength, and nobility. The congregation sings, "With awe and deeply bowed, we praise th'incarnate God...." At the final strains, "We our thank off'rings bring, and grateful sing praise to our heavenly King," every candle is raised high, the benediction is given, and the service quietly concludes.

CANDLES IN THE NIGHT

At one time, the Moravians' apothecary, succeeded by Simon Rau and Company Drug Store, was located just across the church green from Central Moravian Church. For two special Christmases, 1936 and 1937, then-owner Robert A. Smith placed three beeswax candle trees—one large, with 38 candles, and two small, with 9 candles each, in the window of the drug store closest to the church. A silhouette of the church belfry was placed behind the largest candle tree. On Christmas Eve of those two years, as Mr. Smith saw the church darken, and then softly glow with candles from the multiple flames, he would light the 56 candles on the trees and darken the store. As the worshippers left the service, the massed glow of candles gleamed from the store window.

Today, his son, Robert W. A. Smith, continues to make the candle trees for retail sale. He and his wife, Lucille, sometimes give costumed demonstrations of beeswax candlemaking and trimming and display antique molds. They are members of Central Church.

"MORNING STAR"

In Moravian Christmas services, it is not at all unusual to find the same hymns sung year after year. Each has become, over many years, a tradition in its own right. One in particular is "Morning Star," a beloved fixture in the Moravian Christmas Eve Vigils as well as in the Vespers of both Moravian College and Moravian Academy in Bethlehem.

In his collection, *Christmas Traditions: Bethlehem, Pennsylvania*, the late Dr. Richmond E. Myers, professor emeritus of Moravian College, wrote, "One (Moravian anthem) in particular has found such a permanent place in the affections of many folk that it is used far beyond the confines of the Moravian denomination. This is 'Morning Star,' written by Johann Scheffler, who lived from 1624 to 1677."

The words were first set to music believed to be Christian Gregor's 310th meter, arranged by Johann Freylinghausen in 1704. The tune so familiar to us today was composed in 1836 by Francis F. Hagen, who graduated from Moravian College in 1835.

Moravian College Vespers have included the performance of "Morning Star" since the late 19th century. Moravian Academy, which serves pre-kindergarten through 8th grades on its Lower School campus in Bethlehem, and 9th through 12th grades at its Upper School campus in Bethlehem Township, also includes "Morning Star" as an honored tradition in its Christmas Vespers. Moravian Academy is the oldest private school in America.

THE CHILD SOLOIST

The clear, sweet voice of the child soloist begins each verse of "Morning Star," while the congregation echoes the words. Moravian churches near and far have performed this antiphonal song since the 19th century.

It is common in late fall to find prominent coverage in Bethlehem area newspapers announcing the selection of the "Morning Star" soloist for each of the six Moravian College Vespers, the two Moravian Academy Vespers, and the three

CALM REPOSE
High above a gathering of about 1,100 participants, the child soloist mounts a platform near the balcony railing to perform.

Central Church services on Christmas Eve. The selection is, after all, a prestigious event. The child chosen has auditioned for the honor and may be either a male or female 5th grader between the ages of 10 and 11. Of utmost importance is that the voice be a soprano; thus, the boys who audition do so before their voices change to the lower range.

Amazingly, the children chosen are also noteworthy in their calmness, for each young child who performs in the Vesper and Vigil services in Central Moravian Church must mount a platform near the balcony railing carrying a lighted candle and perform the four verses of the song high above a gathering of about 1,100 participants. There is often a family reputation to uphold as well, since it is not unusual for a chosen child to be preceded in this honor by one or more older siblings.

The clear, sweet voice of the child soloist begins each verse of the song, while the congregation echoes the words. As late as 1912, records show that the anthem was sung by the soloist and children of the congregation only, but today, all ages, both choir and congregation, join in the antiphonal rendering of this cherished piece.

While the exact process may vary from one Moravian church to another, one constant remains: The effect is always beautiful and impressive.

THE MORAVIAN TROMBONE CHOIR

The Bethlehem Moravian Trombone Choir holds the distinction of being the most unique musical organization in existence today. It is the oldest group of its kind in continuous existence in the United States and, likely, the world.

Trombones have been associated with the history of the Moravian Church since the early days of Herrnhut. The first record of these instruments being used in America was in August of 1754, when they were used in Bethlehem's Festival and Prayer Day of the Unmarried Brethren. Since that date, only slide trombones have been used in Bethlehem, in soprano, alto, tenor, and bass voices. Until 1765, all the trombones in this country were in Bethlehem. At that time, two other sets were introduced from Europe into other Moravian communities.

TROMBONES

Trombones have been associated with the history of the Moravian Church since the early days of Herrnhut. Their first appearance in America was in Bethlehem in 1754.

THE RENOWNED TROMBONE CHOIR

The Choir uses only trombones in multiple sizes, including a soprano in the same key as the trumpet, and an F bass built in 1889. An extra attachment enables the player to reach the seventh position. The choir's more than two dozen members represent varied Protestant denominations and include several women.

On December 2, 1792, two sets of trombones were used in Bethlehem to announce the death of Bishop Augustus G. Spangenberg, a prominent Moravian leader. However, the trombones remained a novelty outside Moravian communities. In 1822, the Musical Fund Society of Philadelphia needed three trombones for a performance of Haydn's *Creation*. Since there were none in Philadelphia, three players were summoned from Bethlehem. They quickly became the center of attention because few people had ever seen a trombone.

On Christmas Eve, 1913, the trombone choir was again called to Philadelphia, to play for the lighting of Philadelphia's first Christmas tree. Three chorales were played from the top of Independence Hall.

The Moravian Trombone Choir continues to play an important role in Bethlehem's celebration of Christmas. Literally, the choir opens the season for the city annually. It is their honor to play the prelude at the Community Advent Breakfast on the Saturday before the first Sunday of Advent. The next afternoon, the trombones call participants to worship at the annual Advent Lovefeast of Central Moravian Church. Occasionally, they play for holiday services at other Bethlehem area Moravian churches.

On Christmas Eve at Central Church, following the prelude, the sound of the trombones is heard softly in the distance playing the hymn "Briesen," or "All My Heart This Night Rejoices." Traditionally, the trombones play the opening selection from the attic above the sanctuary, 60 feet above the worshippers.

On New Year's Eve, they hold a distinctive advantage in the 11:30 P.M. worship hour. At the stroke of midnight, the trombones sound forth with the strains of "Now Thank We All Our God," announcing that it is midnight, and a New Year. Since the pastor's sermon precedes the midnight hour, it is not unusual for the address to be interrupted in mid-sentence—one of our more unusual Moravian traditions!

A Christmas Eve much earlier in time is remembered for the trombones interrupting a more urgent occurrence in Bethlehem history. According to legend, a war party of Native Americans camped opposite

Bethlehem on Christmas Eve of 1755, planning a dawn attack on the Moravian settlement. At the same time as they were crossing the Lehigh River to commence their attack, the trombone choir had climbed to the roof of the Brethren's House (now the Music Department of Moravian College) to welcome Christmas Eve with traditional Moravian chorales. The Native Americans, hearing the mellow notes of the trombones, were frightened off, thinking that the strange sound was the voice of their Great Spirit, warning them to turn back.

Records show that the Native Americans were, indeed, on the warpath at that time, and it is a known fact that the trombonists did play from the roof of the Brethren's House to announce church festival days, such as Christmas Day. The tale of that particular happening reportedly reached Bethlehem the following summer, either by way of the missionary that converted a member of the war party or by the convert himself. While the church diary does not record any direct reference to the occurrence, J. Mortimer Levering does note in his *History of Bethlehem, Pennsylvania* the interesting fact that on that particular day, the trombones announced the Christmas morn at 4:00 a.m., rather than at their customary time of 5:00 a.m. One may only speculate whether the settlers had become aware of the potential attack, and thus, steps may have been taken to rouse them at an earlier hour. To quote the late Richmond E. Myers in his collection, *Christmas Traditions: Bethlehem, Pennsylvania*, "...there is no positive historical proof that the trombones saved Bethlehem from an Indian attack. On the other hand, there's no proof that they did not."

A TROMBONIST PLAYS

The Moravian Trombone Choir plays an important role in Bethlehem's celebration of Christmas. It provides the prelude at the Community Advent Breakfast and at Central Church's Advent Lovefeast. On Christmas Eve, the members can be heard high above the sanctuary, in the church's attic, playing "All My Heart This Night Rejoices."

Edgeboro Moravian Congregation
645 Hamilton Ave. Bethlehem, Pa. 18017
PLEASE
KEEP IN COOL PLACE
CONTENTS:
Powdered sugar, water, food coloring and flavor extract.

SUGAR, SPICE, AND EVERYTHING NICE

More than at any other time of year, the holiday season prompts a flurry of activity in area kitchens and bake shops, as traditional cakes, cookies, and candies are prepared. Moravian sugar cake, Lovefeast buns, paper-thin rolled cookies, and mints are abundantly in evidence.

If a Moravian family were entertaining guests, knowing that they'd be expected to serve sweets that were typically "Moravian," chances are that the dessert of choice, served with coffee or tea, would be Moravian sugar cake. This classic yeast bread is usually baked in square pans and may be purchased in that fashion throughout the year at the Moravian Book Shop and other Bethlehem bake shops. A raised bread, or coffee cake, its dough traditionally contains potatoes. When the dough has risen and is ready for baking, indentations are made in the top with the thumb, and butter is placed in each hole. Cinnamon and brown sugar are sprinkled over the entire top before baking.

Another traditional Moravian treat at Christmastime is Moravian ginger thins. Those skilled in the intricacies of making these paper-thin cookies often use a chilled slate to roll the cookies. Many, however, prefer to purchase them at the Moravian Book Shop, which orders them from Old Salem, North Carolina. Referred to in that southern Moravian community as "Christmas cakes," the paper-thin ginger cookies originated there in 1760, and it is from there that they are distributed throughout the nation.

MORAVIAN MINTS

One thousand completed boxes of mints in four colors are sold to the Moravian Book Shop for the holiday season and to visitors to the Edgeboro Community Putz. According to the labeling on the boxed mints, they use "a traditional Moravian recipe handed down from the Candymakers of Colonial Bethlehem."

For those who prefer the "sugar high" of pure confectioners' sugar mixed with only water, food coloring, and flavoring,

SWEET TREATS ARE PREPARED FOR HOLIDAY SALE
Moravian mints are a special Christmas treat made by the women of Edgeboro Moravian Church, who have carried on the tradition for at least 75 years.

Moravian mints are a Christmas treat often served to guests or taken along to friends' homes as a hospitality gift. Edgeboro Moravian Church of Bethlehem has carried on this candy-making tradition for at least 75 years. More than two dozen makers and packers gather each week for four or five weeks in October and November, spending two days making and two more days packing their peppermint, spearmint, wintergreen, and anise mints of pink, green, white, and yellow. Each batch must be hand-stirred for a full 30 minutes. Once poured, the drying of the mints takes 12 hours. The 1,000 completed boxes of mints in all four colors are then sold to the Moravian Book Shop for the holiday season and to visitors to the Edgeboro Community Putz. This labor of love originated with women of Edgeboro Church. According to the labeling on the boxed mints that are sold, they use "a traditional Moravian recipe handed down from the Candymakers of Colonial Bethlehem."

Also favored during the holidays by Moravians and other Pennsylvania Germans are sand tarts, anise drops, almond or currant cakes, springerle cookies, and APEAS cookies, which have the initials "AP" carved into the tops.

THE MORAVIAN BOOK SHOP

The Moravian Book Shop has been part of Bethlehem's history since 1745 and is recognized as the oldest book shop in America, and probably, in the world. Anchoring the lower, or southern, end of Main Street, its vast expanse has grown in recent years. Books share company with tempting gourmet foods, delicious deli goods, charming gifts, decorations for the home, traditional Moravian items, greeting cards, paper products, and much more. Most recently, the book department doubled in size, with an entire section devoted to children's books, complete with a children's reading room. A section has also been added for CDs and cassette tapes.

CHRISTMAS LIGHTS GLOW
The delightful window displays of the Moravian Book Shop, lighted trees, and Victorian street lamps enhance the holiday atmosphere for shoppers.

The Moravian Book Shop was founded in 1745, when the Moravian Church appointed Samuel Powell of the Church's

(continued on page 44)

THE MORAVIAN ROOM

This expansive section of the shop houses an enchanting array of Moravian memorabilia and Christmas items: trees, ornaments, pottery, beeswax candles, and Moravian stars of paper and glass.

ORNAMOTION

Crown Inn, south of the Lehigh River, to operate a bookstore.

After several locations, the shop was moved to the church's publications building near Central Moravian Church in 1871. It remains there today, but it has expanded both to the north and south of its earlier site, spilling into store after store in that immediate area. The result is a wondrous collection of distinctive merchandise displayed in most attractive architectural and decorative settings.

During the Christmas season, the Moravian Book Shop is an especially enchanting wonderland and a "must-visit" destination for out-of-town visitors. An entire section of the store is devoted to Christmas decorations, Moravian Stars and candles, and other representations of the Moravian influence in Bethlehem.

While today's Moravian Book Shop bears little resemblance to its original concept, its ties to the Moravian Church are still strong and beneficial. Owned by the Moravian Church and governed by a Board of Directors, it plays a vital role in Bethlehem's economy. Through great effort, it has reached the age of more than 250 years, and it continues to thrive. Its proceeds are designated to support the Ministers' Pension Fund of the Northern Province, helping to support retired Moravian ministers, widows, and widowers.

HOLIDAY CHARM

Unique items such as this delightful nutcracker, Santa, and figurines of carolers please shoppers searching for the perfect gift. Many more reflect the Moravian influence in Bethlehem.

PART II

Bethlehem's Celebration of Christmas. . .

. . .and Its Moravian Influence

BETHLEHEM AS "CHRISTMAS CITY USA"

Each Christmas, visitors come from all over our country, from Canada, and from abroad to visit Bethlehem of Pennsylvania, known through much of the world as Christmas City USA. Some come to absorb the Moravian heritage of this community, formally named in a Christmas Eve service in 1741. Others rediscover the true meaning of Christmas as viewed in the Moravian putz, the Live Bethlehem Christmas Pageant, and the Nativity figures at City Center Plaza. All appreciate the quiet beauty and dignity of a monthlong celebration that begins on the first Sunday of Advent with the illumination of thousands of tiny white and colored lights throughout the city.

For much of the 20th century, the Bethlehem Area Chamber of Commerce played an important role in the city's Christmas celebration. In 1936, the idea for lighting the city was born, when Vernon Melhado, then-president of the Chamber, said, "Why not make Bethlehem—named at Christmas—the Christmas City for the entire country? Bethlehem did not create Christmas, but Christmas created Bethlehem."

It was in December of 1937 that Bethlehem first attracted nationwide attention through a massive Chamber effort. A home-lighting contest was begun on December 1 of that year, sponsored by the Chamber, to encourage Bethlehem residents to reflect the city's spirit through their home exteriors. Two days later, letters were sent to 2,500 Chambers of Commerce across the country asking each to notify their local newspapers of the effort to make Bethlehem "the Christmas City." It was suggested that people

VICTORIAN MAIN STREET GLISTENS
Bethlehem's Main Street is a magical sight during the Christmas season. Tiny white lights glow from the street's natural trees, from Christmas trees mounted on lampposts, and from shop windows. Victorian street lamps add to the charm.

Above

SHOP WINDOWS OFFER ALLURE

Main and Broad Streets in the north side Historic District are lined with charming shops, boutiques, and restaurants. Their holiday-trimmed windows offer enticing glimpses of the unique offerings to be found within.

At right

CHRISTMAS CITY CANCELLATION

The Bethlehem Post Office on Wood Street hand-cancels nearly a half-million Christmas cards each year as special requests. The senders may choose to have either the Star of Bethlehem or the wise men appear on the cards.

Opposite page

A CANDLE IN EVERY WINDOW

Windows in shops, businesses, and homes reflect warmth and hospitality to all that pass by. It is one of Bethlehem's most endearing Christmas traditions.

throughout the nation send their Christmas cards to Bethlehem to receive the "Christmas City" cancellation. Nearly 1,800 Chambers cooperated and more than 185,000 pieces of mail soon flooded the city's post office.

Today, the Bethlehem Post Office on Wood Street hand-cancels nearly a half-million Christmas cards each holiday season as special requests. The cancellation can bear either the Star of Bethlehem or the wise men.

While today, Bethlehem refrains from decorations that cry of glitz and glitter, in those early days one might say that the city glowed with glitz. Strings of lights with stars and bells paraded across Main Street above the trolley tracks and continued across the Hill-to-Hill Bridge. It was much bigger than anything we have today, and lines of cars clogged Main Street with traffic as residents and visitors alike took in the dazzling sights.

By 1960, some thought that the lighting had gotten out of hand, and the Citizens' Christmas City Committee was formed under the auspices of the organization that had created all the glitz to begin with: the Bethlehem Area Chamber of Commerce. Charged with bringing a sense of dignity to Bethlehem's lighting displays, the committee has accomplished that, and raises a great deal of the funds needed to support the lighting through its program of Christmas City Seals initiated in 1965 and Christmas City Cacheted Covers, which were introduced in 1983.

In addition, the Citizens' Christmas City Committee is responsible for the Community Advent Breakfast and the Community Tree-Lighting Ceremony, held annually on the weekend of the first Sunday of Advent.

BETHLEHEM: MINDFUL OF ITS RELIGIOUS HERITAGE

This Christmas, like every Christmas, people will come from near and far, from many states and foreign countries, to visit our museums, take our nighttime lantern and bus tours, experience the Moravian Community Putzes, hear the beautiful Christmas music, and shop our many unique stores and boutiques. A common thread is woven through the tapestry that makes up Christmas in Bethlehem. It is one of dignity, and of being ever mindful of the city's religious heritage.

The first tradition of the season takes place on the Saturday before the first Sunday of Advent, when several hundred Bethlehem area residents gather for a Community Advent Breakfast, held annually since 1965. Each year, either a local member of the clergy or a lay person is invited to give an address. Choral music is also featured. The Moravian influence surfaces each year in the form of a prelude by the Bethlehem Moravian Trombone Choir, the presence of Moravian sugar cake as part of the ample breakfast, and the lighting of beeswax candles at the event's conclusion, combined with the singing of "O Little Town of Bethlehem." Perhaps one of the strongest evidences of Bethlehem's religious heritage is the fact that its extensive lighting display is not turned on until the evening of the first Sunday of Advent. In recent years, a concession has been made to that hard-and-fast rule: limited lighting of the trees in the business districts on the day after Thanksgiving.

AN ENCHANTING SIGHT ON CHURCH STREET

Each Christmas, 16 evergreen trees, 12 to 14 feet in height, are purchased to line Church Street in front of the city library. Dressed in snow and tiny Christmas lights, they add to Center City's enchantment.

On that first Sunday of Advent at dusk, many hundreds attend the annual Community Tree-Lighting Ceremony, which features a rotating schedule of high school choruses and prominent community choirs. Outstanding local high school bands

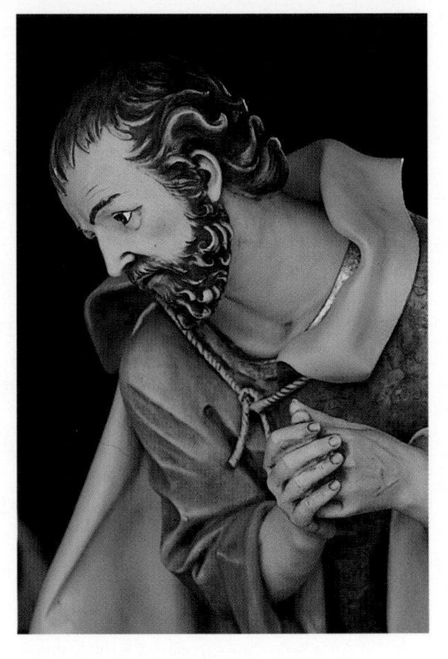

THE NATIVITY

The Nativity scene in City Center Plaza was purchased by the Citizens' Christmas City Committee for Bethlehem's 250th anniversary in 1991. The hand-painted ceramic figurines were imported from Italy and depict the Holy Family and related figures. This scene replaces the committee's original set of life-size figures that stood in that spot. It is now on view each holiday season in front of Christ Church, United Church of Christ, on Market Street.

provide assistance, and a special child is chosen each year to help Bethlehem's mayor set the lights aglow. Once again, the Moravian influence is remembered as voices join in singing "Jesus, Call Thou Me," sung by those first Moravians on Christmas Eve of 1741. Even the Bethlehem Post Office on Wood Street joins in the spirit by hand-canceling all Christmas cards brought to the ceremony with the Christmas City station postmark, including the date of the first Sunday of Advent and the belfry of Central Moravian Church.

Held in City Center Plaza, surrounded by massive Christmas trees and with the Star of Bethlehem shining from South Mountain across the Lehigh River, it is a simple ceremony marking the advent of the Christmastide.

Still other reminders of Bethlehem's religious heritage have become an integral part of the city's Christmas decorations. Displayed prominently in City Center Plaza is a nearly life-size Nativity scene, with its figures nestled in a stable lined with hay. Nearby is one of the four imposing Advent wreaths, each with its four massive electric candles, placed on or near bridges throughout the city. The highest candle in each wreath towers 15 feet into the air. Each Sunday of Advent, one of the four candles is lighted until, by the Sunday before Christmas, all four glow in the evening darkness.

ADVENT CANDLES BURN

One of the city's four imposing Advent wreaths is on view at City Center Plaza. One candle is lighted on each of the four Sundays of Advent. The tallest candle in each wreath towers 15 feet into the air.

BETHLEHEM: ITS MUSICAL HERITAGE AND TRADITIONS

Bethlehem is truly a city steeped in musical traditions, and many of them center on the celebration of Christmas. Once again, this varied chronicle of musical excellence began with Bethlehem's early Moravians. When they came to America, they brought with them their musical culture. From the beginning, these people were noted for their performing of music as a wonderful way to glorify the Lord. Wherever they went, the Moravians took their hymnals, their instruments, and their manuscripts of choral and instrumental music.

Early Moravians composed as many as 3,000 pieces of music, possessing the largest collection of music used in the colonies. This talented community also crafted many fine musical instruments, resulting in an active and sophisticated musical culture. The Moravians' reputation for instrument building, accomplished composition of choral and instrumental works, performances of European masterworks, and formation of musical groups provided Bethlehem with the reputation as a most prestigious place to make music, according to Moravian records of the 19th century.

A gratifying evidence of Moravian musical culture may be found in the fact that Haydn's oratorio "The Creation" was rendered for the first time in America in Central Moravian Church in 1811. The church earned its status as a National Landmark of Music after Bach's masterpiece, Mass in B Minor, was presented there in 1900, the first complete performance of that work in America.

To this day, the love of sacred music in the classical style is characteristic of Moravian descendants. Since its founding, Central Moravian Church has set a standard for both musical

COLLEGE VESPERS
Beeswax candles are raised high at the conclusion of the Moravian College Vespers. The six annual services held each December in Central Moravian Church draw more than 1,000 students, parents, faculty, and alumni to each.

expression and performance of spiritual compositions.

Today, Christmas concerts abound from the Central Church campus to churches, schools, and choral groups throughout the Bethlehem area. Many of them have become traditions of their own. Recognized here are a few that have endured for a number of years and have become cherished events of the Christmas season.

Following the tradition established in 1742 by Bethlehem's first school, Moravian Seminary for Young Ladies, its successor, **Moravian College**, continues the custom of holding an annual Christmas service. For several decades, these have been held in Central Moravian Church and have greatly expanded. In 1957, the concerts took their present form of anthems and hymns that relate the Christmas story through Scriptures, and the lighting of beeswax candles. The six annual Moravian College Vespers draw more than 1,000 students, parents, faculty, and alumni to each, with only a small number of tickets remaining for the general public.

Lehigh University, founded in 1865, counts among its favorite traditions the Christmas Vespers, with a candlelight procession of chorus members, carol singing, and, as long as anyone can remember, the inclusion of the familiar hymn, "Lo, How a Rose E'er Blooming."

Bethlehem's **Liberty High School**, which began presenting Christmas Vespers in 1922, now sustains the holiday tradition in the form of a Winter Concert. Its Alumni Chorus, formed at the time of the school's 75th Anniversary in 1997, carries on the original tradition of the school's Christmas Vespers.

Since **Freedom High School** opened its doors in 1967, it has held an annual Winter Holiday Concert. While a variety of sacred and secular music is included, several parts of the program remain constant. Near the conclusion of the program, the gowned choral groups process with candles to the carol "Once in Royal David's City." After combined choral pieces with orchestra, the program traditionally concludes with the "Hallelujah Chorus" from Handel's *Messiah*, followed by a candlelit recessional to another carol, "Lay Down Your Staffs."

In the 1751 Old Chapel, Bethlehem's second place of worship, **Music in the Old Chapel** draws both passersby and bookings of charter bus groups to the series of late-afternoon concerts held weekdays throughout December. Since 1986, it has been a welcome respite, featuring prominent Lehigh Valley organists, guest soloists, and group caroling. The historic chapel is located just a few steps from Central Moravian Church.

Candlelight Concerts are also a popular event for out-of-town bus groups and for the general public, presented in the chapel of Christ Church, United Church of Christ, Saturday and Sunday evenings at 6:00 P.M. They offer a step back in time as talented artists present early Moravian compositions and other music of the season.

Handel's *Messiah*, by the **Cathedral Choral Society** of Cathedral Church of the Nativity, has been performed in Christmas concerts since 1964. The Society observes its 50th anniversary in the year 2000. The *Messiah* Singalong, performed annually at Salem Lutheran Church, has been a cherished tradition since 1976.

The **Bach Choir of Bethlehem**

GUEST ARTISTS
Central Moravian Church's Christmas Eve Vigils are enhanced each year by the Philadelphia Brass, the Concerto Soloists of Philadelphia, and the Moravian College music faculty.

A STANDARD OF EXCELLENCE
The 55-voice choir of Central Moravian Church is noted for its standard of excellence as it performs anthems in English, German, and Latin.

Christmas concerts have been an institution since only 1984, but the choir itself has been a legend in the community for more than 100 years. It was organized in 1898 by J. Fred Wolle, organist at Central Moravian Church at that time. Through its century of excellence, the Bach Choir of Bethlehem has gained international recognition. Among its concert recordings are several that highlight its repertoire of both classical and classic Christmas music.

Other Bethlehem area groups, such as the **Concord Chamber Singers** and **St. Luke's Singers** of St. Luke's Hospital, join in maintaining a tradition of high quality in holiday choral music.

THREE CENTURIES OF HISTORY AND A VERY SPECIAL CHRISTMAS

Many visitors who tour Bethlehem during the Christmas season are intensely interested in knowing more about the city's heritage, its early founding by the Moravians. Thus, thousands of those who travel into the city by tour bus or by car plan to spend some time in Bethlehem's museums. Each year, these sites offer greater opportunities for learning more about Bethlehem's early Moravian history. It is good fortune, indeed, that all but one of the museums are an easy walk within the city's Historic District.

MUSEUMS WELCOME VISITORS
The 1810 Goundie House is just one of Bethlehem's center-city museum sites that welcomes visitors during the holidays.

Most are operated under the umbrella of the Historic Bethlehem Partnership. At the Moravian Museum, one may tour the 12 rooms of the 1741 Gemeinhaus (Community House), the oldest building in existence in Bethlehem and in

At left
A MINIATURE PUTZ
Each holiday season, a Christmas putz, or miniature Nativity scene, may be found nestled in the fireplace of the Moravian Museum's Music Room. Some of the Nativity figures are at least a century old.

Below
A CHILD'S HOLIDAY DREAMS
A vignette of dolls and toys loved by all ages includes Polly Heckewelder (at right), made by the Ladies Sewing Society of Central Moravian Church since 1872.

Opposite page
OH CHRISTMAS TREE
In one particular holiday exhibit, the Moravian Museum highlights Christmas trees through the ages.

continuous use by the Moravians through the present time. Here, visitors gain an accurate picture of 18th-century life in the settlement of Bethlehem and the history of the Moravian church itself. There is always a small Christmas putz nestled in a fireplace, a tree trimmed with such simple adornments as beeswax candles and spice cookies, and early Moravian dolls and toys.

In the Colonial Industrial Quarter, the 1761 Tannery and the 1762 Waterworks (the first municipal pumped water system in the American colonies) open their doors to visitors. Interpreters explain the Moravian settlement's burgeoning industrial growth and give children the opportunity to become involved with simple craft projects and with the HistoryWorks! Gallery in the 1869 Luckenbach Mill.

On Main Street, the 1810 Goundie House is exquisitely decorated for the holidays and includes displays of antique clothing. It was once the home of the local Moravian brewmaster, John Sebastian Goundie, and his family, and is believed to be the first brick residence in Bethlehem.

Kemerer Museum of Decorative Arts, also in the Historic District, is gloriously bedecked in Christmas finery throughout its spacious rooms that occupy two adjoined Victorian houses. Visitors can view several magnificent Christmas trees trimmed in period styles. Throughout the

1762 WATERWORKS

The 1762 Waterworks houses the machinery for the first municipal pumped water system in the American colonies. The exterior was restored in 1976. The Waterworks is a National Historic Landmark.

museum, two centuries of high-style furniture plus folk and decorative art are on display. At this site, the Moravian influence is present in the paintings of Gustav Grunewald, who came to Bethlehem in 1831, taught drawing and painting at the Young Ladies' Seminary from 1836 to 1866, and left a legacy of many oil paintings depicting Bethlehem scenes before returning to Europe in 1868. The works of other early Moravian artists are also displayed here.

Those who visit the 1758 Sun Inn will be greeted as cordially as guests were in the 18th century—guests that included George Washington, John Hancock, the Marquis de Lafayette, Ethan Allen, and John Adams. Visitors may savor the ambiance of an 18th century tavern, with its *Gaststube* (guest suite), bedroom suite, and old kitchen.

A short distance from Center City is Burnside Plantation, being restored as an historical farm museum. The 1748 farmhouse and reconstructed 1841 Pennsylvania bank barn give visitors a glimpse of history as lived when James Burnside, a Moravian missionary, farmer, and political representative, became the area's first private landowner.

For those who wish to further understand the Moravian Church and its beginnings, there is the spectacular multimedia three-screen production, *Mission: Bethlehem—It All Begins with Christmas.* Through stirring narration, visuals, and music recorded in Bethlehem by the

(continued on page 68)

Above

1810 GOUNDIE HOUSE

During the holidays, Mrs. Goundie, wife of 19th-century Moravian brewmaster John Sebastian Goundie, may be found helping visiting children make gingerbread cookies in her kitchen.

At right

LANTERN TOURS

Guides in 18th-century Moravian costume lead visitors on evening lantern tours of the 1741 Gemeinhaus, 1752 Apothecary, and 1758 Nain House, ending with refreshments at the 1758 Sun Inn.

Opposite page

1761 TANNERY

The 1761 Tannery in the Colonial Industrial Quarter opens its doors to visitors on holiday weekends. Restored in 1971, the massive limestone building holds exhibits on early leather production as well as other colonial crafts and trades.

Above left
KEMERER MUSEUM
A covering of snow intensifies the mood for viewing the holiday visions that await visitors to the Kemerer Museum of Decorative Arts.

Above right
MEMORIES OF CHILDHOOD PAST
Young and old alike delight in changing holiday exhibits such as this one of cast-iron toys at the Kemerer Museum. Dazzling Christmas trees, dolls, and decorative arts spanning three centuries are on display.

Opposite page
1758 SUN INN
This gem of 18th-century Moravian architecture has welcomed townspeople and visitors since 1760. Today, its first-floor rooms serve as a living history museum. Delicious luncheons and dinners may still be enjoyed in the second-floor dining room.

Moravian College Choir, the Bach Choir of Bethlehem, and the 500th Anniversary Festival, the vision, love, and strength of Bethlehem's early Moravian settlers is recalled.

Each day, there are walking tours of the Historic District and on many evenings, lantern walking tours. On Church Street, visitors are privileged to see America's largest collection of original Germanic buildings, still occupied today by Moravians and by students of Bethlehem's Moravian College and Moravian Theological Seminary. In the evening, each window of these massive limestone structures glows with the quiet beauty of a single candle.

Again, it is fortunate that in Bethlehem, one may easily walk the area that encompasses the Historic District. One may hear the clip-clop of horses' hooves as visitors take nostalgic carriage rides. Or, in another favorite pastime, visitors may stroll Victorian Main Street and be enchanted by the myriad shops, boutiques, and eateries with their charming, white-lighted window displays. Bethlehem welcomes one and all to experience its three centuries of history—and its very special Christmas.

THE STAR ON SOUTH MOUNTAIN

Just as the star led the shepherds and wise men to Bethlehem long ago, another star welcomes visitors today—those who come each holiday season to see the thousands of lights and learn about the rich heritage found in Bethlehem of Pennsylvania. Positioned high atop South Mountain, the Star of Bethlehem is the largest known display of its kind in the world, visible for 20 miles to the north, limited by hills and the Earth's curve in its long-range visibility to the south.

From the city, the display appears as a conventional five-pointed star, with eight rays emanating outward. From a distance, it appears as a traditional shepherd's star with a bright center mass, hovering over the community. Its main vertical ray is 81 feet high; the main horizontal ray, 53 feet across.

The Star of Bethlehem represents more than the Christmas season. Its symbol has been incorporated into the official city seal. Each of the five points represents a major facet of the city's character—religion, education, music, industry, and recreation. Bethlehem's rich heritage began with the Moravians and has been perpetuated by the ethnic, cultural, and industrial diversity that has followed.

Since 1935, the Star of Bethlehem has stood. First built of wood, it was rebuilt with galvanized steel from Bethlehem Iron Works in 1936, then redesigned in 1967. The imposing steel and Plexiglas structure has become a permanent tradition. Its 246 lightbulbs are changed every two years so that they continue to shine brightly.

Until the mid-1990s, the star was lit only during the Christmas season. At that time, the decision was made that the star would remain lighted year-round, a reminder to all that Bethlehem is the Christmas City.

A WELCOME TO VISITORS
Two hundred and forty-six lightbulbs illuminate the star that appears as a conventional five-pointed symbol with eight rays emanating outward. This image was used for the 1989 Christmas City Seal.

NIGHT LIGHT BUS TOURS

Once more, one of Bethlehem's most popular Christmas traditions originated through the Moravian Church. Tourism officials call these tours "the ONLY way to see Bethlehem."

In the late 1940s, when Bethlehem's lighting returned to its most dazzling after World War II, the city's Rotary Club asked Miriam Taylor and Jeanette Zug, associated with the Moravian Museum, to organize tours that would show off the lighting. Mrs. Zug trained young people of the Moravian Congregation to board tour buses at the Hotel Bethlehem at the foot of Main Street and conduct guided tours of the city, ending with a visit to the Central Church Putz.

Other individuals played key roles in later years until the early 1970s, when the Bethlehem Area Chamber of Commerce took over the organization of the tours. By the early 1990s, the Bethlehem Tourism Authority had assumed this role.

A guide in early Moravian attire accompanies the one-hour bus tour on a ten-mile route. Through a fascinating narration, passengers are led on a journey spanning three centuries of the city's history. Viewers pass the Mayor's Tree, the city's only display of colored lights on the north side. Church Street is next on the route, transitioning from the modern City Center Plaza with its Nativity scene, to 18th-century Moravian buildings. A history lesson accompanies the tour as it passes through the Historic District. Then, the bus crosses to Bethlehem's south side, and soon it is climbing South Mountain, where passengers are able to glimpse the huge superstructure of the Star of Bethlehem that sheds its beams across the Lehigh Valley. The pause atop the mountain, looking down at the shimmering

DECORATED SPLENDOR
A magnificent lighted tree of 40 feet or more takes center stage on the Hill-to-Hill Bridge each holiday season, donated by a Bethlehem area resident. The familiar lighted belfry of Central Moravian Church stands as a sentinel at the entrance to Main Street.

Christmas lights of the city below, is literally the high point of the trip for most, and a dramatic way to catch the holiday spirit. As the bus descends the steep hillside and the city lights stretch out before their eyes, the group often sing "O Little Town of Bethlehem," a most appropriate moment in the trip.

Night Light Bus Tours are offered numerous times each night through the Advent and Christmas season. Because of their popularity, visitors are wise to book these tours in advance.

Above

NIGHT LIGHTS AND HISTORY, TOO

Guides in early Moravian attire accompany the popular Night Light Bus Tours on a ten-mile route. Passengers view the city's Christmas lights from the Historic District to the Star on South Mountain, and are led on a narrative journey spanning three centuries of Bethlehem's history.

At left

CHRISTMAS TREES ABOUND

The Citizens' Christmas City Committee purchases 775 Christmas trees to adorn lampposts throughout the Historic District and main arteries into the city. The committee works closely with city electricians, who string the thousands of tiny lights.

SEALS, CACHETS, AND CHRISTMAS BALLS

Throughout each and every year, the Citizens' Christmas City Committee of the Bethlehem Area Chamber of Commerce works closely with the city's electrical department to support the maintenance and expansion of Bethlehem's widespread Christmas lighting. In 1965, the committee began a custom that continues today: the use of Christmas City Seals to support the cost of the lighting programs.

THE CACHETED COVER
This envelope, similar to a first-day cover, is of special interest to stamp collectors. It features that year's postage stamp of the Madonna and child, the Christmas City Seal, and special postmark.

Early each November, seals are mailed to 10,000 members of the community. The design changes annually and is chosen from those submitted by local artists that may include painters, photographers, and graphic designers. In turn for the seals, residents and businesses loyally contribute more than $20,000 annually to support the city's Christmas lighting.

BETHLEHEM'S MOST FAMILIAR LANDMARK
The towering belfry of Central Moravian Church has appeared on the Christmas City Seal or the Cacheted Cover numerous times.

The strength of the Moravian influence on the community is particularly evident at Christmastime. The city's most identifiable landmark, the towering belfry of Central Moravian Church, has appeared in the Christmas City Seal 11 times in the years between 1965 and 1999, while another Moravian historic building or symbol has been a seal subject an additional 12 times in those 35 years.

Since the inception of the Christmas City Cacheted Cover introduced in 1983, the same subject is chosen for both the seal and cacheted cover in any given year. The latter is of particular interest to stamp collectors. Since 1983, the Central Church belfry or another Moravian subject has appeared ten times on a cacheted cover, through the year 1999.

Another item of interest to collectors of Bethlehem memorabilia is the Limited Edition Christmas Ball. These keepsakes were introduced in 1989 by the Bethlehem Area Chamber of Commerce to help support the work of the Chamber. Central Moravian Church was its first subject, and that year's ornament remains the most popular-selling ball of the series. Each year, a historic Moravian building has been chosen as the subject, and the ornaments continue to be collectibles that will be passed down and cherished through generations.

LIVE BETHLEHEM CHRISTMAS PAGEANT

In a city laden with traditions, the Live Bethlehem Christmas Pageant is one of the most unique. It originated when the Rev. Leonardo Iacono, of Our Lady of Pompeii of the Most Holy Rosary Catholic Church on Bethlehem's south side, brought an Italian custom to the Christmas City. With the help of his sister, Brigida, they brought to Bethlehem the reenactment of the birth of Jesus with a costumed cast of characters, music, and caroling.

CHRISTMAS PAGEANT
This annual presentation on a weekend in December is one of Bethlehem's more charming holiday traditions. It originated in 1978 and is carried on each year by a realistic cast of volunteers.

On Christmas Eve of 1978, the pageant was presented on church grounds and in surrounding streets. Since then, it has centered around the Community Arts Pavilion, which adjoins the south campus of Moravian College. As a community event, Bethlehem residents John and Nancy Cornish guided the

THE ENTRY OF MARY AND JOSEPH
How many times we have heard the Christmas story told, but never more believably than in the roles reenacted by the cast of the Live Bethlehem Christmas Pageant.

pageant together for the first 20 years, and Cornish continued his leadership after his wife's passing in 1999.

Each year at 2:00 P.M. on a Saturday and Sunday in mid-December, the public is invited to dress warmly, bring a chair, and gather for the pageant. Miraculously, the pavilion is transformed into a stable for that event. Down a steep hillside nearby, Joseph guides a donkey as it makes its agile way to the stable, bearing Mary on its back. During the next hour, shepherds, angels, wise men on real live camels, soldiers on horseback, assorted livestock, and hundreds of citizens dressed in period costume make their way to the manger where a real baby lies. There is music and narration, once again retelling the age-old Christmas story.

The pageant committee spends much of the year gathering costumes and making arrangements for this special event. While principal characters are cast in advance and there is minimal rehearsal, much of the cast is gathered at the last minute. An appeal is made through the local newspapers, inviting residents and out-of-town visitors to just "show up" an hour before the rehearsal, when they will be assigned a part and appropriately costumed.

How many times we have heard the Christmas story told, but never more believably than in the roles reenacted in the Live Bethlehem Christmas Pageant. Its realistic presentation truly reminds us of Christ's coming, and the real reason for the season.

BETHLEHEM: A TAPESTRY OF CHRISTMAS TRADITIONS

For the first 100 years of Bethlehem's existence, it remained a closed communtiy. Visitors were welcome, but only Moravians could live here. The church and the town leaders were one. For that century and a few years more, the settlement's traditions remained relatively undisturbed.

Then, in 1845, the Moravians began to permit others to purchase property. In a passage from *Bethlehem of Pennsylvania: The Golden Years 1841–1920*, *"A burst of activity shook the quiet and measured life of the people. Men and women from other parts of the valley and the nation and from other countries entered and made homes. They joined in the work of fashioning the wealth of the earth into usable products, improving the means of transportation and building a new sort of industrial economy."*

THE STAR SHINES BRIGHTLY Visible for 20 miles to the north of the city, the star shines brightly from its position high atop South Mountain.

At right
A BIT OF TRIM
Fresh greens and red bows dress the Victorian street lamps on Bethlehem's Main Street.

Opposite page
ETHNIC TREES
A display of ethnic Christmas trees greets visitors to the Comfort Suites, Bethlehem. The project, which features trees dressed in holiday ornaments representing more than a dozen countries, is sponsored annually by the South Bethlehem Historical Society, Comfort Suites, and participating ethnic churches and organizations.

And so it was that, following the Civil War, the entrepreneurs entered Bethlehem, establishing the Bethlehem Iron Works (later Bethlehem Steel Corporation), the Lehigh Valley Railroad, and other businesses and industries that would need vast numbers of workers to help build the economy. By the late 19th century and early 20th century, waves of immigrants had come to the city to find work, setting up neighborhoods and churches, principally on Bethlehem's south side.

The first of these came from Ireland, England, and Germany. Later, they came from Eastern Europe: the Czechs, Slovaks, Hungarians, Slovenes (or Windish, as they are known in Bethlehem), and Ukrainians. Italians and Greeks came, as well as Portuguese, Spanish, Serbs, Croatians, Lithuanians, Turks, and Romanians. Among the last to come were the Mexicans and Puerto Ricans. The majority were Roman Catholic, but some were of the Lutheran or Reformed denominations. Still others belonged to the Russian Orthodox or Greek Orthodox churches.

Thus began Bethlehem's melting pot of various cultures blending one into another. Ultimately, there emerged new and totally different Christmas traditions, brought to the city by these many divergent nationalities from their own homelands, just as the Moravians had brought their special customs with them more than a century before. What had been a church village for many long years was now undergoing the monumental changes wrought by the Industrial Revolution. But still, simple Christmas traditions—stories, beliefs, and customs—handed down through generations would blend together and give Bethlehem its distinctive ethnic diversity.

During the Christmas season, one is mindful of this diversity while attending the Community Tree-Lighting Ceremony, as the city's six-ton Symbol of Progress made of Bethlehem Mayari R steel, looms 60 feet above the heads of those gathered. It was erected to symbolize the many different ethnic groups on which the city is based. The statue soars upward and inward to show the integration of Bethlehem's people, then progresses skyward to illustrate how its people have been strengthened by their diverse beginnings and their subsequent meetings.

As residents and vistors travel through Bethlehem during the Christmas season, they are reminded by tour guides that the white lights decorating the city's north side represent the Moravian heritage brought here by those first settlers, while the multicolored lights that adorn the south side are thought of as representing the ethnic diversity of many more who came from many nations to help make this city great.

And thus, each Christmas season, Bethlehem is known not only by its Moravian traditions but also by a multitude of ethnic traditions—religious, historic, musical, and familial. Just a few of the city's many traditions from many lands are illustrated through. . .

- ▲ Christmas in South Bethlehem: An Ethnic Experience, an exhibit of ethnic Christmas trees at Comfort Suites, South Bethlehem.
- ▲ The Live Bethlehem Christmas Pageant, an Italian custom brought to Bethlehem in 1978.
- ▲ Vespers and Christmas Carols, a service in English followed by carols sung in Russian at St. Nicholas Russian Orthodox Church.
- ▲ Las Posadas, originating in Mexico and observed by the Hispanic community beginning nine days before Christmas. The Baby Jesus is carried from home to home seeking shelter; on the day before Christmas, the live Nativity scene assembles at Holy Infancy School.
- ▲ Holiday appearances by St. John's Windish Lutheran Church and St. Joseph's Slovenian Catholic Church combined choirs in their native costumes.
- ▲ Guest appearances by members of the community at nationally recognized Touchstone Theatre's performances of "Christmas City Follies." The community guests share with the audiences their own personal experiences of cultural diversity from their memories of Christmases past.

Today, the Allentown-Bethlehem-Easton area is a burgeoning megalopolis, a thriving center of business and industry known as the Lehigh Valley. At its hub lies Bethlehem, steeped in not one but many Christmas traditions, old and new. It is a city of lights, of history, of welcome to travelers from near and far. It provides a home for more than 70,000 residents, weaving their rich diversity of traditions into a tapestry that is Bethlehem, unique in its stature as Christmas City USA, unique because this vast city was once a tiny frontier settlement, founded by a devout Protestant denomination, the Moravian Church.

"...each wave of immigration, generation of people, and technological advance has reshaped a pattern that began (over two hundred and fifty years ago), adding to, supplementing, amalgamating with it, but always only in part, to produce a balance of peoples and cultures imperfectly harmonizing with an older tradition."

Bethlehem of Pennsylvania: The First One Hundred Years 1741–1841

BETHLEHEM AREA MORAVIAN CHURCHES

Advent Moravian Church, **3730 Jacksonville Rd., Bethlehem, PA 18017**

Pastors: The Rev. Gordon B. Mowrer, The Rev. Ronald Rice
Office: (610) 866-1402
Church: (610) 868-0477
Fax: (610) 868-0507

Special Christmas Observances
Tree-Lighting Ceremony, first Sunday of Advent, 5:00 P.M.
Anniversary Lovefeast, Sunday closest to December 11, 8:30 A.M., 10:45 A.M.
Christmas Eve Children's Lovefeast and Candle Service, 5:00 P.M.
Christmas Eve Candle Service, 8:00 P.M.

Central Moravian Church, **Main and W. Church Sts., Bethlehem, PA 18018**

Pastors: The Rev. Dr. Douglas W. Caldwell, The Rev. Peter D. Skelly, The Rev. Carol A. Reifinger
Office: (610) 866-5661
Fax: (610) 866-7256
E-mail: central@enter.net
Web site: www.enter.net/~cmc/

Special Christmas Observances
Advent Lovefeast, first Sunday of Advent, 3:30 P.M.
Lessons and Carols, third Sunday of Advent, 9:00 A.M. in the 1751 Old Chapel;
11:00 A.M. in the church sanctuary
Christmas Eve Children's Lovefeast, 1:00 P.M.*
Christmas Eve Vigils, 5:30 P.M., 8:00 P.M.*
Christmas Day Worship Service, 11:00 A.M.

** Free tickets must be obtained for all three Christmas Eve services. Send a stamped, self-addressed envelope to the Central Moravian Church office, 73 W. Church Street, Bethlehem, PA 18018.*

College Hill Moravian Church, **72 W. Laurel St., Bethlehem, PA 18018**

Pastor: The Rev. Carol P. Dague
Office: (610) 867-8291
Fax: (610) 865-3067
E-mail: chmcbeth@juno.com
Web site: www.enter.net/~rharney/chmc.htm

Special Christmas Observances
Advent Lovefeast, first Sunday of Advent, 10:45 A.M.
Sunday School Christmas Program, third or fourth Sunday of Advent, 10:45 A.M.
Christmas Eve Family Lovefeast and Candlelight Service, 4:00 P.M.
Christmas Eve Candlelight Service, 8:00 P.M.

East Hills Moravian Church, **1830 Butztown Rd., Bethlehem, PA 18017**

Pastor: The Rev. Gary Marsh
Office: (610) 868-6481
Fax: (610) 868-6219

Special Christmas Observances
Advent Lovefeast, first Sunday of Advent, 11:00 A.M.
Holy Communion, second Sunday of Advent, 8:30 A.M., 11:00 A.M.

Annual Sunday School Christmas Pageant, third Sunday of Advent, 11:00 A.M.
Christmas Eve Children's Lovefeast, 4:00 P.M.
Christmas Eve Lovefeast and Candle Vigils, 7:30 P.M., 10:00 P.M.

Edgeboro Moravian Church, **645 Hamilton Ave., Bethlehem, PA 18017**

Pastor: The Rev. Kerry Krauss
Office: (610) 866-8793

Special Christmas Observances
Christmas Musicale, fourth Sunday of Advent, 10:45 A.M.
Christmas Eve Children's Lovefeast, 4:00 P.M.
Christmas Eve Candelight Services, 6:00 P.M., 8:00 P.M.

West Side Moravian Church, **402 Third Ave., Bethlehem, PA 18018**

Pastor: The Rev. Aden Ward
Office: (610) 865-0256
Fax: (610) 865-0256
E-mail: westsidemoravian@juno.com

Special Christmas Observances
Children's Lovefeast, first Sunday of Advent, 7:00 P.M.
Christmas Eve Candle Vigil, 7:30 P.M.
Christmas Day Worship Service, 10:00 A.M.

MORAVIAN COMMUNITY PUTZES

(All three are open to the public during the hours* listed and are closed December 24 and 25.)

Central Moravian Church

First Sunday of Advent: 1:00–3:00 P.M., 5:30–8:30 P.M.
December 1–23: Wednesday through Saturday, 4:30–8:30 P.M.
Sunday, 1:00–8:00 P.M.
(closed Mondays and Tuesdays)
December 26–30: Daily, 1:00–8:00 P.M.
December 31: 1:00–10:30 P.M.
Group tours by appointment; call the church office at (610) 866-5661

East Hills Moravian Church

December 1–31: Monday through Friday, 6:00–8:00 P.M.
Saturday–Sunday, 3:00–8:00 P.M.
Group tours by appointment; call the church office at (610) 868-6481

Edgeboro Moravian Church

December 1–30: Daily, 6:00–8:00 P.M.
Group tours by appointment; call the church office at (610) 866-8793

** Days and hours subject to change from year to year; call the above-listed numbers to verify.*

REFERENCES

Adams, Marcia. 1992. *Christmas in the Heartland.* Clarkson Potter Publishers.

Bynum, Flora Ann L. 1983. *The Christmas Heritage of Old Salem.* The Williamsburg Publishing Company.

Fries, Adelaide L. 1973. *Customs and Practices of the Moravian Church.* Board of Christian Education and Evangelism.

Levering, J. Mortimer. 1903. *History of Bethlehem, Pennsylvania.* Times Publishing Company.

Myers, Richmond E. 1985. *Christmas Traditions: Bethlehem, Pennsylvania.* Acorn Graphics division of Oaks Printing Company.

Nelson, Vernon H. 1990. *The Bethlehem Gemeinhaus: A National Historic Landmark.* Oaks Printing Company.

Sawyer, Edwin A. 1990. *All About the Moravians: History, Beliefs and Practices of a Worldwide Church.* The Moravian Church in America.

Schattschneider, Allen W. 1956, 1990. *Through Five Hundred Years.* The Moravian Church in America.

Stocker, Harry E. 1918. *Moravian Customs and Other Matters of Interest.* Times Publishing Company Printers.

Yates, W. Ross et al, eds. 1968. *Bethlehem of Pennsylvania: The First One Hundred Years 1741-1841.* The Bethlehem Chamber of Commerce.

Yates, W. Ross et al, eds. 1968. *Bethlehem of Pennsylvania: The Golden Years 1841-1920.* The Bethlehem Chamber of Commerce.